IFEYINWA FREDERICK

Ifeyinwa Frederick began writing in 2016, joining Soho Theatre Writers' Lab. *The Hoes* is her debut play and was shortlisted for The Tony Craze Award and Character 7 Award and longlisted for the 2017 Verity Bargate Award. She writes alongside her full-time job as co-founder of Chuku's, the world's first Nigerian tapas restaurant, which has seen her featured in Forbes' list of 100 Women Founders in Europe.

Mike Bartlett
ALBION
BULL
GAME
AN INTERVENTION
KING CHARLES III
WILD

Jez Butterworth
THE FERRYMAN
JERUSALEM
JEZ BUTTERWORTH PLAYS: ONE
MOJO
THE NIGHT HERON
PARLOUR SONG
THE RIVER
THE WINTERLING

Caryl Churchill
BLUE HEART
CHURCHILL PLAYS: THREE
CHURCHILL PLAYS: FOUR
CHURCHILL: SHORTS
CLOUD NINE
DING DONG THE WICKED
A DREAM PLAY after Strindberg
DRUNK ENOUGH TO SAY I LOVE YOU?
ESCAPED ALONE
FAR AWAY
HERE WE GO
HOTEL
ICECREAM
LIGHT SHINING IN
    BUCKINGHAMSHIRE
LOVE AND INFORMATION
MAD FOREST
A NUMBER
PIGS AND DOGS
SEVEN JEWISH CHILDREN
THE SKRIKER
THIS IS A CHAIR
THYESTES after Seneca
TRAPS

Fiona Doyle
ABIGAIL
COOLATULLY
DELUGE
THE STRANGE DEATH OF JOHN DOE

Natasha Gordon
NINE NIGHT

debbie tucker green
BORN BAD
DEBBIE TUCKER GREEN PLAYS: ONE
DIRTY BUTTERFLY
EAR FOR EYE
HANG
NUT
A PROFOUNDLY AFFECTIONATE,
    PASSIONATE DEVOTION TO
    SOMEONE (– NOUN)
RANDOM
STONING MARY
TRADE & GENERATIONS
TRUTH AND RECONCILIATION

Vicky Jones
THE ONE
TOUCH

Anna Jordan
CHICKEN SHOP
FREAK
POP MUSIC
THE UNRETURNING
YEN

Arinzé Kene
GOD'S PROPERTY
GOOD DOG
LITTLE BABY JESUS
MISTY

Lucy Kirkwood
BEAUTY AND THE BEAST
    with Katie Mitchell
BLOODY WIMMIN
THE CHILDREN
CHIMERICA
HEDDA after Ibsen
IT FELT EMPTY WHEN THE
    HEART WENT AT FIRST BUT
    IT IS ALRIGHT NOW
LUCY KIRKWOOD PLAYS: ONE
MOSQUITOES
NSFW
TINDERBOX

Nessah Muthy
HEROINE
SEX WITH ROBOTS AND
    OTHER DEVICES

Amy Ng
ACCEPTANCE
SHANGRI-LA

Janice Okoh
EGUSI SOUP
THREE BIRDS

Nina Raine
CONSENT
THE DRUNKS after Durnenkov
RABBIT
STORIES
TIGER COUNTRY
TRIBES

Sam Steiner
KANYE THE FIRST
LEMONS LEMONS LEMONS
    LEMONS LEMONS

Jack Thorne
2ND MAY 1997
BUNNY
BURYING YOUR BROTHER IN
    THE PAVEMENT
A CHRISTMAS CAROL after Dickens
HOPE
JACK THORNE PLAYS: ONE
JUNKYARD
LET THE RIGHT ONE IN
    after John Ajvide Lindqvist
MYDIDAE
THE SOLID LIFE OF SUGAR WATER
STACY & FANNY AND FAGGOT
WHEN YOU CURE ME
WOYZECK after Büchner

Phoebe Waller-Bridge
FLEABAG

Ifeyinwa Frederick

THE HOES

NICK HERN BOOKS
London
www.nickhernbooks.co.uk

A Nick Hern Book

The Hoes first published in Great Britain in 2018 as a paperback original by Nick Hern Books Limited, The Glasshouse, 49a Goldhawk Road, London W12 8QP, in association with Hampstead Theatre

The Hoes copyright © 2018 Ifeyinwa Frederick

Ifeyinwa Frederick has asserted her moral right to be identified as the author of this work

Cover image: istockphoto.com/PeopleImages

Designed and typeset by Nick Hern Books, London
Printed in the UK by Mimeo Ltd, Huntingdon, Cambridgeshire PE29 6XX

A CIP catalogue record for this book is available from the British Library

ISBN 978 1 84842 799 0

Woodland
CARBON
www.woodlandcarbon.co.uk
NICK HERN BOOKS
Printed on Carbon Captured paper

The Hoes was first performed at Hampstead Theatre Downstairs, London, on 26 October 2018. The cast was as follows:

ALEX	Aretha Ayeh
BIM	Marième Diouf
J	Nicola Maisie Taylor

Director	Lakesha Arie-Angelo
Designer	Anna Reid
Lighting	Jai Morjaria
Sound	Duramaney Kamara

Characters

ALEX, *twenty-five, black, from Essex*
BIM, *twenty-five, of Nigerian heritage, from Essex,*
    a self-proclaimed hoe
J (*Jasmine*), *twenty-five, black, from Essex*

/ – indicates that the line is spoken at the same time as the next character's speech or as the next stage direction is acted out.

// – indicates where a character's speech should continue straight through without a break whilst stage directions or other character's lines happen at the same time.

Note on Play

All three girls grew up in Essex and attended the same all-girls secondary school and have been friends since their early teens. They are extremely comfortable with each other. Remarks that might seem catty if said by someone else are between them a sign of how close they are. Similarly, they are extremely comfortable with their own and each other's bodies and are tactile in a non-sexual way.

They are adherents to half-naked dressing and their wardrobe throughout is made up of bikinis, short skirts, short dresses, crop tops, short shorts and other fitted outfits. All their outfits are carefully put together, and though not wearing much they are always well-dressed and never look 'cheap'.

They are away for a girls' holiday in Ibiza where a group of boys from home are also on holiday. The girls' accommodation space includes a kitchen and bathroom but all onstage action takes place in the girls' bedroom, where they share a bed.

Growing up in the late nineties and noughties, they've got a love for UK garage, Sean Paul's countless chart hits, the early days of grime and girl bands from Spice Girls to Girls Aloud. As young adults, having spent many a Friday night dancing to the likes of Calvin Harris, Duke Dumont and Jax Jones, they've now also developed a love for the house beats and dance music Ibiza is famed for. Music used in or in between scenes reflects the girls' personal tastes.

Scene changes should reflect the Ibiza atmosphere – club lights, heavy beats and excited energy.

This text went to press before the end of rehearsals and so may differ slightly from the play as performed.

Scene One

*It is the third full day of the girls' holiday. They have been there
for three nights already. 3 p.m. Tulisa's 'Young' is playing in the
background. J is in the bathroom. ALEX and BIM are sat on
one of the beds drinking rosé out of mugs. They also have a
bottle of Sambuca, vodka and bottle of a mixer. They are dressed
in the clothes they slept in. Matching pyjamas is not a thing for
the girls. Pyjamas for them consist of T-shirts, shorts, long strap
tops – anything that covers them without outdoing the benefits of
air-conditioning. The room looks lived-in, messy, though not
dirty. Not wanting to unpack, they use their suitcases as their
wardrobe, which their clothes are now spilling out of and clothes
they have previously worn or have tried on and discarded are
also all over the room. Make-up and hair accessories are also
out. There is a makeshift money jar somewhere in the room,
visible to the audience, and there are already some euros in it.
The girls are supposed to be getting ready to go out, though
drinking has taken precedence over actually getting dressed.
BIM is drinking at a faster pace than ALEX, who nurses the
same drink throughout their conversation.*

ALEX. Had he finished?

> BIM *is silent.*

> So, you literally just got up and ran? Did you even say bye?

BIM. Did I even know his name? He didn't need a bye.

ALEX. I'm actually done.

BIM. I was too, that's why I left.

ALEX. What do you think he did after?

BIM. Probably called me a hoe and finished himself off whilst
dreaming about still being inside me.

ALEX. You are…

BIM. When in Ibiza... Might stay off the tequila rosé today though. I can't handle those shots like I used to and I don't wanna make it a habit.

ALEX. The one-night stands or the running after sex?

BIM. The latter.

ALEX. The alcohol didn't make you run, Bim. That was all you.

BIM. True, but I only ran once the alcohol wore off and he started to look a lot less like Drake than I remembered. And in fact, if it wasn't for the shots you made me do I would have chosen someone actually good looking. So really this is all on you. You deprived Mr 'I Don't Know His Name' of his big finish. So how did you sleep last night?

ALEX. Pretty well, actually.

BIM. I can imagine. All that masturbation must tire you out.

ALEX*'s face says 'what?'*

Babe, every day you're in there – (*Gesturing towards the bathroom.*) doing – (*Imitates the sound of a vibrator.*)

A guilty silence from ALEX.

Missing his tongue, are you?

BIM *pretends to push a head down to her groin and starts making pleasure sounds as if she's receiving oral sex.*

Ah, yes, right, there.

ALEX. Shut up!

BIM. Why are you acting like all the time you spend at his, you're sat watching Disney? If he's not eating you out at least twice each time you visit, you should ask for a refund on your Uber fare.

ALEX. Bim!

BIM. His lips were made for it. It's only fair.

ALEX. That is my boyfriend you're talking about.

BIM. A fact is a fact.

BIM *pours herself another drink.* ALEX *goes to speak but stops herself.* BIM *picks up on it.*

Go on. What?

ALEX. Promise you won't get mad?

BIM. I'm Nigerian. I can't promise you that. Fire runs in my blood.

ALEX *sighs.*

Just say.

ALEX. I think… well, I was wondering… maybe you should slow down.

BIM. Are you the alcohol police?

ALEX. No, I meant with men. Just that guy you did a runner on, he's the third one you've slept with since we got here.

BIM. And?

ALEX. We've only been here three nights.

BIM. So, I have a hundred-per-cent success rate.

ALEX. And then there's Chris.

BIM. That's different. We're friends.

ALEX. And you've had sex with plenty of your 'friends'.

BIM. Not ones like Chris I haven't. We're actual friends and you know this. Think about how long I've known him. He was there for every essay crisis and actual crisis at uni. I don't think he can be put in the same category as those other guys.

ALEX. Fair point. But I'm just saying, we've been friends since before you even knew how to write an essay and you wouldn't even kiss me during a drunken game of spin the bottle. Yet you and Chris have –

BIM. I haven't slept with him.

ALEX. Yet.

BIM *is silent.*

Look, I just –

BIM. This is me, Alex. This is what I do. I like men. I like sex.

ALEX. I know. And you know me. A couple of years ago I would have been joining you.

BIM. Exactly!

ALEX. I just don't want you doing it for the wrong reasons.

BIM. My vagina wanting it isn't good enough a reason for you?

ALEX. That's not what I –

BIM. Look, just because you've opted to have one dick inside you for the rest of your life doesn't mean I have to join you.

ALEX. Bit dramatic, Bim. We're looking at flats, not engagement rings. And that's not even...

BIM *is now clearly ignoring* ALEX.

I just wanted to make sure you're okay. It's just. It's only been a few months since... Y'know, you've literally only just started your –

BIM. Which I don't actually need.

ALEX. Okay, but you've admitted you need your sessions and you're still having them.

BIM. And they have nothing to do with what goes on in my vagina.

ALEX. Is that true?

BIM *ignores her and makes a point of topping up her drink.*

Look, I promised your mum I'd look out for you.

BIM. I'm twenty-five, Alex! I don't need babying. I have told you I'm fine. Now, please, can you just let me enjoy my holiday. That's all I want. Please?

ALEX. Okay. Okay. I'm sorry. I won't bring it up again. Just be careful.

BIM. I've got Durex, I've got Magnum, I've got Skyn. Don't worry, I'm careful.

ALEX. That's not what I meant.

BIM. Don't worry, I've heard you. Now can we get back to what we do best?

BIM *tops up* ALEX*'s drink and shouts towards the bathroom, opening another bottle.*

J, hurry up! You're missing out. We're starting another bottle.

ALEX. Yeah, how long are you gonna be in there for? Some of us actually need the toilet.

J (*offstage*). Just come in, it's not like I haven't seen it before.

ALEX. I need a dump. I don't think you want to be in there for that.

BIM *makes sounds of disgust.*

J (*offstage*). One sec!

J *enters with her phone in her hand.*

I've gotta say, I can see why I attracted so much attention last night. (*Showing off her body.*) Look at me.

ALEX (*getting up to go to the toilet*). Finally!

J. You should have just come in.

ALEX. You should have just come out.

J. I was occupied, Alex.

ALEX *exits.* BIM *looks at* J *expectantly.*

What?

BIM. You promised us. No business calls or emails on holiday.

J. But I –

BIM. No buts, J. You agreed. It's a euro each time. C'mon, add it to the jar.

J. But you're wrong. I was selfie-ing.

BIM. For half an hour?

J. The lighting in there isn't great. It took me a while to find the right spot.

BIM. Sure your Instagram fans will appreciate your diligence.

J. These photos aren't for posting. Can't have pictures like these circulating the internet.

BIM. And who are you sending those kinds of photos to?

J. Nobody. (*Admiring her chest.*) But my boobs looked extra good today. Had to capture that. A little pick-me-up for when self-doubt creeps in. Some people say affirmations. I look at pictures of myself.

BIM. So you just have a catalogue of nudes at the ready?

J. Yup. I'll show you. I'm pretty proud of my collection.

BIM *and* J *sit down on the bed.* J *finds the gallery on her phone and starts scrolling through, showing* BIM. BIM *takes the phone to look more closely at a couple. She's clearly impressed.*

BIM. Damn, J. You're –

J. I know, right.

BIM. I'm jealous. I just can't take a good photo. Even with a filter, I never look better than a four out of ten. And well, we both know that's not true.

J. Mmm… I've seen your Insta. It's shocking. You're like the only person that looks better in real life than online.

BIM. I know. It's damaging my brand. And y'know there is an unmet demand for naked pictures of me but anything I take always makes my boobs look too far apart.

J. Angles, Bim, all about angles.

BIM. Teach me.

J. Are you serious?

BIM. Yeah. Why not?

ALEX *returns, rubbing her tummy and clearly relieved. She only hears what* BIM *says next.*

I think this could take my sex life to the next level.

ALEX. What are you two talking about?

BIM. Alex, shut the bathroom door! I can smell it from here.

ALEX. My bad.

ALEX *goes to shut the door.*

J. Bim wants me to teach her how to take nudes.

ALEX. This, I have to see.

BIM. Not today, though. We're supposed to be heading out in a bit. We should probably start getting ready soon.

J. I feel too sober to be heading out anywhere. Is it too early to do shots?

BIM. It's never too early for shots.

ALEX. Hold on, you said –

BIM. I said I was off tequila rosé. (*Grabbing a bottle.*) But I didn't say anything about Sambuca.

ALEX. No. I'm not involved.

BIM. Alex, c'mon.

ALEX. Nope. I hate the stuff.

BIM. C'mon, we're on holiday. Plus, we're celebrating.

ALEX. Celebrating?

BIM. Another year and not a single pregnancy scare.

ALEX. Bim, you've never had sex without a condom.

BIM (*pouring out shots of Sambuca and handing them out*). So? They're only ninety-eight per cent effective. And I have a lot of sex. We gots to give thanks. To good sex and being unpregnant.

J. To good sex and being unpregnant.

BIM *holds out a glass to* ALEX. ALEX *stares at her, refusing to take it.* BIM *gives her 'the look'.* ALEX *caves and takes the glass reluctantly.*

ALEX. To good sex and being unpregnant.

They down their shot. ALEX *reacts badly to the taste to* BIM*'s amusement.*

(*To* BIM.) You're actually a witch.

BIM. Birds of a feather flock together, so, if I'm a witch, babe, then so are you two.

J. The three witches of Eastwick.

ALEX. More like the three hoes of Essex.

J. Who are you calling a hoe? I've given up sex, remember.

ALEX. It's been like a week, J.

J. It's been three months.

BIM. But were you not just in the bathroom taking nudes? Someone somewhere is calling you a hoe for that.

J *looks displeased.*

Embrace the title.

J. It's hardly a badge of honour.

ALEX. Depends how you look at it. I quite take pride in it.

BIM. Same. It's a sign I'm living life on my own terms because once you're a woman doing as she pleases with her body, in someone's eyes you qualify for hoe status.

ALEX. Half the time it's not even about how much sex you're having.

BIM (*impersonating a fragrance advert*). Hoe, it's more than just sex. It's a lifestyle.

ALEX *and* BIM *continue their list as if in a fragrance advert.*

ALEX. It's the clothes you wear.

BIM. The way you dance.

ALEX. The pictures you post.

BIM (*speaking normally*). It's an endless list, J.

ALEX. One guy said I was clearly a slut because I wouldn't tell him my 'body count'.

J. Eurgh. I hate that phrase.

ALEX. Trust me.

J. Like why use that to talk about the number of people you've slept with. It sounds more like the number of people you've killed.

BIM. I guess I have killed them in a fashion, with my pus–

ALEX's stomach is starting to play up again and she starts to look uneasy as the conversation continues.

J. Don't.

BIM. Just saying, many men have 'died' on entering my inner thighs. (*Mimicking a male orgasm.*) Oh, Bim, yes, yes!

J. Are you gonna be like this all day?

BIM continues with her 'orgasm' before a bad smell hits her and she stops. J notices the smell too and starts frowning. ALEX exits to go to the toilet. BIM's phone starts ringing as ALEX leaves. J answers it.

Hey… No, it's J. One sec.

J hands the phone to BIM.

It's Chris.

BIM (*on the phone*). Hey, babes, what's up… yep, four at Bora Bora Beach, yeah… Yes, we'll be there on time. We're basically ready.

BIM and J look at each other guiltily, knowing just how unready they are.

Have faith, man… Okay cool, see you then. Bye, babes.

J (*shouting into the phone*). Bye Chris!

BIM hangs up and sits down to pour herself another drink.

BIM. We're never gonna make it for four.

J. Never stood a chance. I don't even know which bikini I'm wearing.

BIM. I hope he knows that. Can't deal with him getting all aggy.

J. He's never gonna get annoyed at you though. He'll blame me or Alex.

BIM. Because?

J. He wants you to sleep with him.

BIM. No, he doesn't.

J (*clearly not believing* BIM). Okay then.

BIM. We've already discussed this and sex isn't part of our arrangement.

J. Bim, he's gone down on you. Last time I checked cunnilingus counted as oral sex.

BIM. Fine. If you're going to be pedantic, penetration isn't part of our arrangement.

J. Well, his eyes were trying to penetrate you last night. Did you not see the way he was looking at you? He's got you on his brain and he wants you on his dick.

BIM. Have you been talking to Alex?

J. No, I'm just observant. Clearly all the fooling around you two have done has whet his appetite. He wants it.

BIM. Even if he did, which he doesn't, there are two people involved here and I –

J. Love sex.

BIM *shoots a look at* J.

You can look all you want but I bet that you two will have sex before we leave. At least once. What happens in Ibiza stays in Ibiza and all that.

BIM. What do I win?

J *looks puzzled.*

You said you bet we'll do it. What do I win if you're wrong?

J. Bring your suitcase.

> BIM *goes to get her suitcase and* J *goes to get her own too. They open them and* J *rifles through the clothes in each case.*

If I'm wrong, you get this.

> J *holds up one of her dresses* (*Dress A*). BIM *assesses it and decides it's a worthy prize.*

But if I'm right and you two have sex, you give me this.

> J *holds up one of* BIM*'s dresses* (*Dress B*).

BIM. Okay, but none of your overly-inclusive definition of sex. Fingers and tongues don't count.

J. Okay, but his penis definitely –

BIM. What about if it's just the tip? Because Ed went in with just the tip and I don't include him on my list.

J. If his dick enters you, Bim, it counts as sex.

BIM. What if he doesn't cum?

J. Still sex.

BIM. What if I don't cum?

J. Shit sex, but it's still sex.

BIM. Right...

J. Sounds like someone's wavering already.

BIM. No. Not even. I just like things to be clear.

J. It's simple, Bim. If Chris's dick goes in, then I win.

> J *holds out her hand to* BIM *for a handshake.*

BIM (*shaking* J*'s hand*). You're on.

Scene Two

Day four. The wagered dresses are now hanging up in the hotel room and remain on stage and visible from this point on. Dress A is by J's belongings and Dress B is by BIM's. *All three girls are in bed, hungover, and again dressed in the clothes they slept in. The mess from the day before remains untouched. None of the girls are on their phone, apart from* J *who is replying to emails and looking at her phone, transfixed.*

ALEX. Were hangovers always this bad?

BIM. They can't have been. I would have stopped drinking as soon as I started.

ALEX. But you're not stopping now.

BIM clearly hears ALEX *but ignores her.*

J (*without looking up*). It's because we're old now.

BIM. Speak for yourself.

BIM peers over J's *shoulder and realises* J *is working. She lets* J *know she knows and points at the money jar.* J *sighs and drags herself out of bed to put several coins in the jar and returns to her position.* BIM *holds out her hand for* J's *phone and* J *reluctantly hands it over.*

J. It's true though. In my card this year, my mum pointed out that now if you round up my age to the nearest ten I'm basically thirty, and if I'm thirty, I'm more than halfway to fifty. We're old.

BIM. In your birthday card? That's fucking depressing.

J. But she had a point. Look at us – debilitated by one night's drinking. If this was us back in Napa we'd be drinking again already.

ALEX. Oh Napa.

BIM. That holiday was so –

J. Messy?

BIM. Yep.

ALEX. Oh my god, remember Johnny Loves Black Girls!

BIM. Who could forget Johnny Loves Black Girls?

J. I think I've got that picture of us and him somewhere.

ALEX. Why did we agree to a picture?

BIM. He was in an 'I Love Black Girls' T-shirt. Some things you need evidence of.

ALEX. I wonder what he's doing now.

J. He's still there.

ALEX *and* BIM. Shut up!

J. It's true. Rochelle's just come back from there.

ALEX. How is your little sister old enough to be going to Napa?

BIM. And how is Johnny Loves Black Girls still going? It's gotta be, what, five years since we were there?

J. Seven. Rochelle's just turned eighteen and there's seven years between us.

ALEX. Fuck off, it was seven years ago.

BIM. Wow.

J. Now you see what I mean. Time… Everything's changed. I'm… We're adults now.

ALEX. I'm not sure I feel much older than the eighteen-year-old me being sick over the side of the boat in Napa. I mean, I definitely vommed last night.

BIM. Yeah but you didn't get any in your hair this time. That's growth.

ALEX. True.

BIM. And just think about the guys we used to talk to then, we'd never be seen dead with any of them now.

J. You'd sleep with them, though. Just in secret.

BIM. Shut up!

ALEX. It's true though.

BIM. Do you think our taste in guys has improved or do guys just get better as they age?

ALEX. It's a hundred per cent the former.

J. Definitely. Guys are still using the 'it's because you're so tight' line when they cum after a second.

BIM. Still?

J. I know. It made me feel eighteen again and not in a good way.

ALEX. I'm sorry but how was eighteen seven years ago?

J. I was still using MSN then.

BIM. I was still a virgin then.

> ALEX *and* J *look at* BIM.

Yes. I was.

ALEX. We must really be talking about a long time ago then.

BIM. We could just as easily be talking about five years ago. I didn't have sex until we were twenty-one, remember. Not like you skanky hoes, giving it up as soon as we hit sixteen.

J. Eighteen. Only Alex did it at sixteen.

ALEX. Look, I'd been horny since fourteen. I couldn't wait any longer.

BIM. You're always horny. See, J. Some things don't change. Nothing to stress about.

J. If it was just Alex's libido, I don't think I'd be bothered.

ALEX. You do remember that you had really shit skin when we were eighteen, J? Now look at you. Your skin is basically flawless, and you're there building your empire. This is your golden age, babe.

J. I've only got two salons – not quite an empire, Alex.

ALEX. Can you hear yourself? *Only* got two salons.

J. But it's true. I haven't made it yet. And sometimes it just feels like life's got more stressful without any of the perks.

Y'know, like if we were back in Napa, I wouldn't be sat here checking emails and getting constant messages from my Aunt Mavis.

BIM. Funny, she's just text you as well. It's a link to some Church Singles' Mingle. (*In an advert voice*.) 'Find God and The One in one night.'

J *looks exasperated*.

ALEX. You know you could just switch off your phone. No emails, no Aunt Mavis. Problem solved.

J. But it's not that simple. That's the problem, I can't just do what I want. Everything has consequences.

BIM. But hasn't that always been life, J, at least to some degree?

J. I guess. It's just I'm working so hard… Like it feels all I do is make sacrifices hoping that it'll pay off one day but…

BIM. It will, J. It has to.

J. And if it doesn't?

BIM *and* ALEX *are silent*.

I just can't help but wonder if I'm doing this right.

BIM. J, you've been featured in three 'thirty under thirty' lists in the last two years. I've only just landed my first real job. I think you're doing okay.

J. But you were busy travelling South America and having adventures. The comparison doesn't work.

BIM. Okay, forget me. But do you know how many people our age would love to be in your position?

ALEX. Bim's right. You need to spare a thought for the rest of us. If this is you doing it wrong then what's doing it right?

J. I guess. Just twenty-five is nothing like I imagined.

ALEX. What did you think it was gonna be? A non-stop party?

J. Kinda. When I bought the flat, I was imagining sex on tap and tequila-rosé-filled weekends. In reality, my vagina's gathering dust and the most exciting drink I have most nights is sparkling water.

ALEX. Nothing wrong with a good bit of sparkling water.

BIM. I'll be honest. I'm listening to all this and I think the solution is quite simple. You need to free the poom poom.

J. What?

BIM. The poom. Free it. All this you're feeling, when did it start?

J. It's been building for a few months.

BIM. And when did you give up sex?

J. Three months ago.

BIM. So one could rightfully assume there's a correlation between this quarter-life crisis and your inactive sex life.

J. I don't think it –

BIM. J, I'm telling you, you need to get laid.

J. I'm not having sex right now, Bim.

BIM. I know. That's the problem. You can say what you like but it's what you want. And it's what would help.

J. There was me thinking we were having an actual conversation and you've managed to make it about sex.

BIM. J, I'm being serious. I've been reading this book, I can lend it to you if you want, it says we feel most powerless when we're focused on all the things we can't change.

J. Right…

BIM. And there's this bit where the author explains how – (*Quoting the book*.) 'we can find liberation in taking control of our controllables.'

J *is lost.* ALEX *is struggling to keep up too.* BIM *realises the girls clearly aren't following.*

(*Pointing at* J*'s vagina*.) One of your controllables, J. You just need to take control. Trust me, sex will set you free. Though maybe try a new position – not everyday doggy.

J. I'd hope I've got more controllables in my life than who goes in and out of my vagina, Bim, but thanks for the tip. I'm gonna shower.

BIM. Seeing as you're getting up can you pass me a bottle? The strawberry and lime one, please.

ALEX. For breakfast?

BIM. Drunk is better than hungover. Easing myself back into it.

J *picks up a can and goes to throw it at* BIM.

Don't throw it. It'll fizz and you know I can't –

J *hears her and throws it anyway –* BIM*'s punishment.* BIM *fails atrociously to catch the can.* J *is about to leave but has one more thing to say.*

J. And I do have sex in other positions. I'm just a very big fan of doggy.

J *leaves for the shower. The girls laugh.* BIM *taps the top of her can a few times to try and reduce the fizz and opens it carefully. She sips some and offer some to* ALEX*, for whom the smell is too much and she jumps out of the bed.*

ALEX. Eurgh, Bim no!

The movement was too sudden for her.

Ow, ow, ow!

BIM. Weak-heart. It's just cider. You're gonna have to get over this soon because we'll be doing it all over again tonight.

ALEX. I'm gonna need some help. Have you got any ibuprofen?

BIM. Yeah, in my suitcase in the zip compartment.

ALEX *goes searching in* BIM*'s suitcase.* BIM *keeps talking paying no attention to what* ALEX *is doing.* ALEX *pulls out an unopened packet of tablets, which she inspects carefully.*

J worries too much, man. You need to teach her how to relax. She'll give herself a heart attack, I swear. Ooh, let's play a game. I saw this thing on–

ALEX (*holding the tablets out so* BIM *can see*). Bim?

BIM. That's not ibuprofen.

ALEX. You haven't even opened them.

BIM. Just put it back.

ALEX. You said you started taking them last month.

BIM. I don't need them.

ALEX. You promised your mum –

BIM. And you promised me you were going to let me enjoy my holiday.

ALEX. Our holiday.

BIM. You know I needed this the most.

ALEX. What you need is to take –

BIM. I'm good, aren't I? Alex, I've got this. I don't need them.

BIM *gets the ibuprofen from her suitcase and hands them to* ALEX, *and takes her prescribed medication back from* ALEX.

Here. These get to work pretty quickly so your head should ease up soon. And then you can join me.

ALEX *takes the ibuprofen from* BIM *and takes two.* BIM *tries to lighten the mood.*

Would you rather have invisibility as a superpower or the ability to teleport?

ALEX. Teleport, every day.

BIM. You're not even tempted by invisibility?

ALEX. Do you know how much money teleportation would save me on Uber?

BIM. Yeah but invisibility! Like, think of all the stuff you could do without people seeing you.

ALEX. But where am I going and what am I doing that I don't want people to see me? It's a weird thing to want as a superpower.

BIM. I just think you haven't given this enough thought.

ALEX. You know I only worry because I care.

BIM (*groans*). Oh I'm so bored of talking about me. Wow. I never thought those words would come out of my mouth.

ALEX. Because you're self-centred.

BIM. True. So let's change it up and let's talk about you. Seize the opportunity. This might never happen again.

ALEX. What about me?

BIM. How's the flat-hunting going?

ALEX. Alright. Haven't found anywhere yet but Stephen says he's lined up a few more viewings for when we're back.

BIM. That's exciting.

ALEX. It is. It's just another thing to think about.

BIM. This is what I mean. We keep talking about me but you've got stuff on your mind. What's up?

ALEX. Just all that stuff J was saying earlier about sacrifices and everything... I mean I can't really relate.

BIM. That's because delayed gratification is a foreign concept to you.

ALEX. You're not helping, Bim.

BIM. Sorry.

ALEX. It's just... I just don't feel like I've got this adulting thing. I mean, I have cereal for dinner most days and sniff my clothes to see if I can get away with wearing them a second or third time. The only remotely adult thing about me is my language.

BIM. That's not true, Alex.

ALEX. Isn't it?

BIM. What about your job?

ALEX. I handed in my resignation the day we left. Consultancy isn't for me.

BIM. You resigned. You never said.

ALEX. I'm saying now.

BIM. What are you gonna do instead?

ALEX. I'll tell you when I know.

BIM. Oh so you haven't... Right. What about the move?

ALEX. What about it?

BIM. Won't you need proof of employment to get somewhere?

ALEX. Oh, I hadn't really thought about that. Maybe we'll find
somewhere before my notice period is up. I dunno, I guess
Stephen and I will have to figure it out when I'm back.

BIM. Are you sure now's the right time?

ALEX. Why are you asking that?

BIM. You just don't seem very...

ALEX. Like I said, I've got a lot on my mind.

BIM. You sure that's it?

ALEX. Yeah. I mean the move makes sense. I guess I'm just a
bit nervous about it. Y'know I've never had to share my
space before. Like even in uni I still had my own room to go
back to. But with this, it won't be my room. It'll be ours,
y'know. It just feels very...

BIM. Adult?

Scene Three

Day five. J and ALEX *have gone food shopping.* BIM *is alone. She is on the verge of a physically violent outburst, clearly agitated. She has been like this for some time, trying and failing to calm herself down. She wants to lash out on herself but is fighting it. She is playing with her hands, aggressively trying to keep them under her control. Her movements become more physically aggressive and she's only just keeping herself under control when someone tries to open the door. It's locked. There's a banging at the door.*

ALEX (*from outside*). Bim, open the door!

BIM. Coming!

> BIM *checks her face looks okay, takes a deep breath and opens the door.*

J. Why did you lock it?

BIM. I didn't want to be disturbed.

ALEX. You better not have touched my vibrator.

BIM. Why would I…

ALEX. Sometimes your fingers just aren't enough.

> ALEX *and* J *crash on their floor and bed, tired from physical activity that wasn't drinking or dancing.*

BIM. Are you not gonna put the food away?

ALEX. Are you?

J. That walk to the shops is too long a walk to do in the sun.

> *All the girls are sat looking at their individual phones.*

ALEX. Ooh… Jade Thompson is having a baby.

BIM. How do you know?

ALEX. She's put the ultrasound photo on Facebook.

> BIM *heads over to* ALEX *to take a look.*

J. Eurgh, I hate it when people do that.

BIM. Well, I'm happy for her. She always looked pregnant so it's good she finally is.

ALEX. Bim!

BIM. What?

J. Oh, today's message has arrived!

BIM *and* ALEX *look at* J *expectantly waiting for her to read it out. She throws her phone to them.*

BIM. 'Hello Jasmine, hope you're enjoying Spain. Do remember to use sunscreen. Believe me, we can get sunburn too. And whilst I would hope you're saving the best of yourself for your husband, I know how excitable you young people can be these days, especially in the sun. But unless you'd be happy with him as the father of your kids do not lie down with him. Enjoy the rest of your trip. Love Aunt Mavis. Kiss.' (*Laughing*.) Love that she signed off the WhatsApp with her name as if you wouldn't know it's from her.

J. I can't even. I'm just grateful it wasn't a Bible Scripture this time.

BIM. Yesterday's one on modesty was brilliant. She'd have a fit if she saw your nudes.

ALEX. I just love that you're here playing Virgin Mary and she's got you down as some kind of Jezebel.

J. Which I'm not.

BIM. Right now.

ALEX. But shouldn't she be happy if you were. Thought she wanted you to have kids soon.

J. Yeah, but she wants me married first. Then I'm to produce the army of grandchildren her kids never gave her.

BIM. Stress.

J. I'm telling you, the woman isn't well. You should have seen the birthday message she sent me this year. Going on about how now I'm twenty-five I need to start thinking about my future and that – (*Clears throat and begins impersonating her Aunt Mavis*.) 'while it's good to see that you have laid the foundations for a successful career, Jasmine, it's about time you look to lay the foundations for a successful family and just like you actively seek business opportunities, begin your active search for a husband.'

BIM. Wow.

ALEX. I can see where she's coming from though.

BIM *and* J *look sharply at* ALEX.

I never said I agree. I was just... I mean, it's the times she grew up in. Think, by our age our parents were married. My mum was already pregnant with me.

BIM. I actually can't think of anything worse. Like if I was Jade, I'd be in tears right now. Pregnant women make me feel sick.

ALEX *and* J. Bim!

BIM. What? It's not my fault. I just see the baby bump and then I think about the whole ordeal. You have no control over your body. Y'know it's nine months of – (*Puffs her cheeks and gestures to indicate being a larger size*.)

J. And swollen feet.

BIM. And then the labour, god, the labour. No. No. No. Even just thinking about it is making me want to vom a little. It's just gross.

ALEX. It's not gross, Bim. It's natural.

BIM. So's taking a dump. Doesn't make my poo any less gross.

J. She has a point.

BIM. Thank you! Props to the women who do it but pregnancy isn't for me. Long live the condom.

ALEX. Even when you're married?

BIM. I don't know about that either to be honest.

ALEX. You don't want to get married?

BIM *shrugs, indifferent*.

J. I can't imagine doing it.

BIM. I know right, one person for the rest of your life. It's a lot.

BIM*'s words preoccupy* ALEX *and, as the conversation turns to her and Stephen's future, she becomes increasingly uncomfortable – though* BIM *and* J *do not pick up on it.*

J. No, you slag, that's not what I meant. Just… well because I've never been in a relationship. The idea is just a bit foreign to me.

BIM. Well, Alex will do it first so she can tell you all about it.

ALEX. Wait, what?

BIM. Well, you're the only one in a relationship.

ALEX. It's been a year. You're a bit premature.

J. Aren't you moving in together?

ALEX. Yeah, but only because it'll save us both some money.

J. Whatever, it's still a big deal. So I don't think Bim's being that premature.

BIM. Thank you. Plus, post-university relationships are different. It's like everything swaps to dog years. So your year is closer to like four years.

J. Is that how dog years work?

BIM. Dunno but it sounded good.

ALEX. I think you're overly invested in mine and Stephen's relationship.

BIM. Someone has to be.

ALEX. Excuse me. I am. Contrary to what you might think I'm not just with him for the sex. He's… It's just easy. Y'know, like when I'm with him everything just feels safe. He's just always there – dependable.

BIM *melodramatically pretends to be sick.*

J. But you just don't see yourself marrying him?

ALEX. That's not what I said. I just… I don't know. I've not really thought about it. I guess I was just seeing how we go. But, we almost can't, can we? I mean, what would I tell the kids about how we got together?

BIM (*begins impersonating an older* ALEX *talking to her children*). 'Well, kids, when your mother was younger she was a horny devil and one day her sexual frustration got too much and she invited your father round for pizza and sex' –

J. Sorry what? I thought you met through mutual friends.

ALEX. We did at Sian's birthday. But we didn't talk loads that night. Then basically there was this one day, it was just before my period, you know how you get super horny just before your period? And I'd always thought he was a little bit hot. He had a something y'know. Anyway, I just thought fuck it. And I messaged him saying, 'I think you're cute, I'd like to get to know you better but I'm too broke to go out, do you wanna come over for pizza and sex?'

J. And he said yes?

ALEX. Pizza and sex, J. Who says no to that? Top tip: have the sex before the pizza otherwise you might be sick while riding.

BIM. You were sick on him? You never told me that part of the story.

ALEX. Almost. All the cheese and pepperoni was threatening to come back up so we swapped to missionary. I definitely squeezed out a silent fart at some point though.

BIM *and* J *laugh and mock* ALEX *for being gross*.

BIM. Seeing as you're oversharing, can I ask, what's it like, Stephen's, y'know?

J. Bim!

ALEX. Sorry, for a second I thought you were asking me about my boyfriend's penis.

BIM. Oh, come on, guys. You're talking to me, remember.

J (*to* ALEX). Are you gonna answer that?

BIM. Why not? It's not like I'm asking for a photo. I'm just curious.

J. About your friend's boyfriend's penis?

BIM. No, about Caucasian genitalia.

J. Given all the guys you've slept with, how have you not explored this for yourself?

ALEX. She doesn't do white guys, remember.

BIM. That's not true. My vagina runs an equal-opportunities policy. Just white guys only approach me to tell me how much they love black girls and I'm not about to have sex with someone so they can tick 'doing a black girl' off their bucket list.

ALEX (*typing on her phone*). Well, Bim, in answer to your question, a Caucasian penis is just like any other penis – just less melanin. For further reading, I direct you to our dear friend, Google.

ALEX *throws* BIM *her phone where she has got up Google images of naked Caucasian men.* BIM *doesn't catch it. She picks it up from where it lands and looks at the pictures in shock. She's clearly a bit disturbed but can't stop scrolling.*

BIM. Stephen can't be this pale. They look like uncooked chicken!

J *and* ALEX *laugh at* BIM*'s shock.*

Don't you ever just look at it and think salmonella?

J. It could just be the lighting. I've had that before – when they're so quick to fire off a dick pic they don't spend time getting the lighting right. Like I even asked for the photo anyway.

ALEX. Alright, Leibovitz.

BIM. Don't mock her, Alex. You haven't seen her nudes. She is the master.

J. Ah, Bim, you're too kind.

BIM. Teach me now. We've got ages till we go out.

J. Okay fine. Top off.

BIM. Actually, I need to warm up.

> BIM *starts looking for a song on her phone to put some music on.*

ALEX. It's not cross-country.

BIM. Shush, Alex. I'm trying to get in the zone.

ALEX (*to* J *but so* BIM *can hear*). I hate it when she gets like this.

BIM (*mocking* ALEX). I hate it when she gets like this.

ALEX. Will you just hurry up and put something on?

BIM. But are you really ready, though?

> BIM *presses play. Spice's 'So Mi Like it' plays.* BIM *starts dancing.* ALEX *and* J *recognise it instantly as the song begins and they start to go wild.* BIM *lets them know this is her moment and* ALEX *and* J *stay where they are, dancing with their bodies from where they're sat, hyping her up. They've shared this song together many times in a club and as the song continues they can no longer resist and join* BIM.

ALL. Skin out my poom poom!

> *As the song plays, they dance as the music commands and the others take turn to respond, cheering each girl on.*

BIM. Okay. I think I'm ready now.

> BIM *starts taking off her top.* ALEX *cheers her on.* BIM *removes her bra with her back to the audience, and the audience never see her topless front. The lesson begins.* ALEX *puts the food away. Meanwhile,* J *is demonstrating the angle at which* BIM *needs to position her body and hold her phone.* BIM *struggles to mimic* J *and takes a few photos that* J *shakes her head at. They try again, this time with* J *helping* BIM *by adjusting her boobs as they go.* BIM *finally gets it. She takes the photo and* J *shows her approval.* BIM *takes a couple more to make sure she's got the hang of it.*

ALEX. How's it going?

BIM *lets* J *know she's satisfied with the photos and* BIM *puts her top back on properly as the following conversation ensues.*

BIM. In another life I would have made a great glamour model.

J. Think your boobs are a bit small, Bim.

BIM. I don't need your negativity in my life.

J. Just keeping it real.

ALEX. Show us then.

BIM *shows* ALEX *one of the photos. She looks equally impressed.*

So, who are you sending that to?

BIM. Good question. So much choice.

J. Sure Chris would love it.

BIM. As I'm sure any heterosexual man would, but no.

ALEX. Why not? He'd give you an honest opinion of your shots.

J. And it's not like he hasn't seen it before.

BIM. That's different. It kinda just happens in the heat of the moment. This is more premediated. Makes it seem there's more of a thing going on, y'know.

J. You play with each other's bits on a regular basis! How is that not already a thing?

BIM. You just don't understand.

J. You're right I don't. (*Grabbing* BIM*'s phone.*) So let's send it.

BIM. Give me back my phone, J!

BIM *chases* J *round the room and the two get physical as* BIM *tries to get her phone back.* ALEX *just watches the drama unfold.* J *all the while continues as if she is about to send the message.*

J. Hmm… what should I say?

BIM. You're not saying anything because you're not sending it.

BIM *bites* J.

J. Oww! Alright. Alright. I was only joking anyway. It's your photo. I wouldn't do that to you. Plus, I can win the bet without cheating.

J *throws the phone to* BIM.

BIM. J, you know I can't…

BIM *clumsily catches the phone, pressing send as she catches it.*

Oh shit.

ALEX. What?

BIM. I sent it.

Scene Four

Day six. BIM *is still out. She went home with* CHRIS *the night before.* J *and* ALEX *are on the bed, hungover. They are in their 'pyjamas'.* J *has just been caught sending work emails again and as the scene begins* J *reluctantly hands her phone to* ALEX *and adds another euro to the jar.*

J. I think I'm dying. About this boat party…

ALEX. We've already paid for our tickets. Plus, I'm not dealing with a stroppy Chris if we cancel last-minute. Y'know he likes to take everything as a personal affront.

J. I'm sure he'll be fine. We'll just hide behind Bim. He'll still be in a good mood with her after those pictures.

ALEX. Bet they made his day.

J. I'm telling you. His message back basically said he wants to sleep with her.

ALEX. That's not what he said.

J. I can read between the lines. I've practically won the bet.

ALEX. Except I think Bim is growing in her resolve.

J *looks doubtful.*

You know what she gets like. She really wants to prove us wrong.

J. I don't know. I just think–

BIM *enters in last night's clothes.*

BIM. J, you've got to help me take some more photos.

ALEX. She's back!

BIM. I said it would take my sex life to the next level.

J. You slept with Chris?

BIM. No! But last night, what his tongue did – it was like discovering a new setting on your vibrator.

ALEX. You don't use a vibrator, Bim.

BIM. Whatever. I think I'm in love.

ALEX. With Chris?

BIM. With his tongue.

ALEX. It was that good?

BIM. Life-changing.

ALEX *and* J. Damn.

BIM. I'm telling you, that photo brought something out of him. He would have stayed in between my thighs all night if I'd told him to – I was the fucking Queen Bee. So, J you need to help me because I want that again.

J. Get in the shower then and class will resume after.

BIM *grabs her things for the shower and exits.* J *looks at* ALEX *confident of her inevitable winning of the bet.*

It's only a matter of time.

ALEX. Maybe you are right. I mean, she said 'life-changing'.

J. I called it.

ALEX. But she seemed pretty adamant about not sleeping with him. I don't get their arrangement but –

J. He's smitten. She has him in the palm of her hand. It's like her ultimate fantasy. When have you ever known Bim to say no to that amount of power?

ALEX (*searching her memory*). Michael the mistake?

J. That's different. He spelt kosher with a 'C'. There was no way Bim was gonna let him put anything in her lady garden.

ALEX. J, please. 'Lady garden'?

J. What?

ALEX. It just sounds so wet.

J. That's what he said.

ALEX (*pointing to her vagina*). This is a powerful thing. If you're not gonna call it what it is, you could at least use a word with more gravitas. Y'know, like cunt.

J. Don't. It's such an ugly word.

ALEX. Lady cunt then.

J ignores her and starts looking at clothes, deciding what to wear. ALEX pretends to be interested in what J is choosing and gets close to J.

(*Shouting in J's ear.*) CUNT!

J. What is wrong with you?

ALEX dances around the room singing 'cunt' like it's a nursery rhyme. BIM enters puzzled by ALEX. As the conversation ensues, BIM gets dressed.

BIM. What is she doing?

J. Winding me up.

ALEX. Giving J alternatives to use instead of 'lady garden'.

J. Winding me up.

BIM. What's wrong with 'lady garden'?

J. Exactly.

BIM. That's what my mum calls it.

ALEX. Exactly. Only women over fifty and writers for *Cosmopolitan* would call it that. (*To* J.) Why won't you just call it what it is? A vagina.

J. I don't like the way it sounds.

ALEX. Well, there's always c–

J *hits out at* ALEX *to stop her finishing her sentence glaring at her until it looks like* ALEX *is going to behave.*

How about pussy?

J. I hate cats.

BIM. See, that one doesn't bother me.

J. Until someone says it to you in bed.

BIM. That's different. Never in bed. It screams 'I'm trying to be sexy.'

J. When it's anything but.

BIM. Has the complete opposite effect.

J. Literally. Nothing makes me dry up faster. It's like anti-lube.

BIM. And it always makes me think the person has watched too much porn.

ALEX. Well, I like it. Especially when it's said breathlessly in your ear. (*Demonstrating how she likes it said.*) Mmm... pussy.

BIM (*pointing at* ALEX). Someone who has watched too much porn.

J. I feel like I just got a window into your and Stephen's sex life that I never wanted.

ALEX *pretends not to hear* J*'s comment.*

BIM. What's it like, the sex?

ALEX. It's like sex, Bim. Penis, vagina, in, out, in, out.

BIM. I know what sex is like, Alex.

J. She's a veteran.

BIM. But this is different. You've been sleeping with the same person and only that person for over a year. What's that like? I just can't imagine it.

J. That's because you're used to sleeping with at least two people a week.

ALEX. More like a day.

BIM. Oh my gosh, guys. One time!

J. Definitely happened twice.

BIM. So, I'm generous. I like spreading joy.

ALEX. You mean your legs.

J *laughs*.

BIM. You still haven't answered my question.

ALEX *is silent*.

Oh, come on, Alex. We're all adults here.

ALEX. Honestly?

J *and* BIM *look at* ALEX *in disbelief that she's even asking*.

I don't know if I can do it for another year.

BIM *and* J *are clearly surprised, caught off-guard by* ALEX*'s honest response*.

J. Is it that bad?

ALEX. No, not at all. It's just one person, the same person, over and over and... I just feel stuck because... well, I do really like Stephen and this last year has been great but sometimes I just wanna have sex with someone else. Y'know, I'm twenty-five... there's a whole world out there I haven't seen. A lot of men I haven't... How do I know that this is the best it gets? I mean, it's pretty good... I'm just... I'm just curious to have someone else inside me. And I don't know why because I chose to be with him. And you're told when you're in a relationship they'll be the only one you ever want, the only one you should want. And everyone's there with all this

'I only have eyes for him' malarkey but... I have eyes for everyone. And I just don't get it. Stephen has revolutionised my vagina in ways I can't describe and we can have the best sex on Sunday but I'll still go to work on Monday wanting Ben from Accounts to eat me out for lunch.

BIM. Who's Ben from Accounts?

ALEX. It doesn't matter. It's not about Ben, Timi... //

J (*mouthing*). Who's Timi?

ALEX. // Or anyone else for that matter. It's me that's the problem.

BIM. So you think about having sex with other people? People that don't are lying. When I was with Mick, I dreamt about sex with his dad all the time.

J. You need help.

ALEX. But it's not like there's just one person I keep fantasising about. I just have this all-encompassing desire for anyone that isn't Stephen.

J. Has it always been like this?

ALEX. No. It was fine in the beginning. Maybe since our anniversary, it was like 'Oh, we're still doing this.' And I swear every time he sends me a flat on Rightmove it only gets worse.

BIM. Maybe you're just not ready to be in a relationship.

ALEX. I am. I just want to have sex outside of it.

BIM. I think you just described being single.

J. Have you thought about talking to him about it?

ALEX. To say what? Hey, I know you're madly in love with me which is great because I really like and maybe love you too, but the thought of sleeping with you and only you for the rest of my life makes me feel a bit anxious so do you mind if I have sex with other people? Nobody wants to hear that.

BIM. You shouldn't beat yourself up about this, Alex. You know you haven't done anything wrong.

ALEX. But I have. A million times in my head. And I am tempted all the time.

BIM. But you haven't actually done anything.

ALEX. I know but –

J. Talk to him.

ALEX. I can't.

J. Alex, this isn't one of these things that will just go away if you put your head in the sand. And yes maybe you'll talk to him and he takes it badly and you two break up. But if you want to stand a chance at making things work, it sounds like something you need to have a conversation about.

ALEX. You're right. And that is probably the adult thing to do. But I'm not you, J, and that's not gonna happen so let's just forget I brought this up.

J. Alex!

ALEX. Conversation over.

Scene Five

Day seven. J is doing ALEX's *hair in the bathroom. The girls are at the very early stages of getting ready to go out.* BIM *is alone in the bedroom. She's on the verge of another violent outburst again and is struggling again to maintain composure. She's already near breaking point and her agitation is clear as she fights to control her hands. It doesn't work, and she silently explodes, throwing what's nearby and hitting her head violently with her hands. The sound of the items she's thrown crashing to the floor is heard in the bathroom.*

J (*from inside the bathroom*). Bim?

The fear of being caught out by the girls breaks BIM's *spell.*

BIM. Was trying to catch my phone – it's nothing.

BIM *breathes deeply and is trying to regain her composure as* ALEX *and* J *enter, oblivious.* J *makes some final adjustments to* ALEX'*s hair.*

ALEX (*showing off her new hairstyle*). Tonight, Matthew, I'm gonna be 'fucking hot'.

BIM. Very nice.

ALEX. Is that it?

BIM. What? I said it looks nice.

J. Nice is verging on an insult. It's just so beige.

BIM. Oh, well I'm sorry my compliment wasn't up to scratch.

J. What's got into you?

ALEX. She's probably cranky because she didn't have any sex last night.

J. True. And you didn't even go home with Chris. Tired yourself out, have you?

BIM. Marathon not a sprint. Sometimes a girl needs a break.

J. And it was well and truly deserved. I don't know where you get the stamina.

BIM. Regular training.

J. I'm thinking of getting a vibrator.

ALEX. Do it. Mine comes everywhere with me.

BIM. Everywhere?

ALEX. Okay not everywhere but you know what I mean. Though I did used to take it to work sometimes and send Stephen videos from the toilet cubicles.

J *and* BIM *display their disbelief.*

BIM. Fucking hell, Alex.

ALEX. That job was so dull, man, I needed to spice up my day.

J. Do you think I can get one out here?

ALEX. Probably, but I'm not sure I'd trust it. It's probably second-hand.

J. Gross!

ALEX. Why don't you just wait until you get home? I'll take you to Ann Summers.

J. Because I'm horny now.

BIM. So why pay for a vibrator when there's men everywhere who can make you vibrate all day long for free?

J. Because I'm not having sex, Bim. We've been through this.

BIM. I thought maybe you'd be over this by now. Three months is a long time.

J. I know! I'm the one doing it.

ALEX. Sounds like masochism to me.

BIM. Love a bit of S&M.

ALEX. How long are you gonna do this for?

J. I don't know. Maybe until I meet someone.

BIM. Fucking hell!

ALEX. So, you're really not gonna sleep with that guy?

J. Which one?

ALEX. Oh, come on, J. The only one. You two manage to find each other every night.

J. No, we're just talking.

ALEX. No one comes to Ibiza to 'just talk'.

J. Not everyone comes for sex, Alex. You didn't.

ALEX. That's true but don't pretend when you and this guy are 'just talking' you're not thinking about what it'd be like to have him on top of you.

J *stutters*.

I rest my case.

BIM. Okay, J, please tell us why are you doing this?

J. I want to be taken seriously.

ALEX. Serious people have sex, J. They just have serious sex.

J. Exactly, serious sex, not casual sex.

BIM. What does that even mean?

J. I... I just don't wanna get left on the shelf. We're twenty-five, if I keep sleeping around for the next few years then...

BIM. Well, I'm sleeping around so what does that mean?

J. I dunno. But don't you ever worry that when you're ready to settle down you might not find someone who'll be okay with... you know, someone who you can be honest with about everything and who'll still respect you.

BIM. Respect me?

J. Numbers matter to most guys.

BIM. They shouldn't.

J. But they do. Like if I went to that Singles' Mingle thing my aunt sent me and we had to wear a badge with the number of people we'd slept with I'd be left in the corner like a leper.

BIM. But you're never gonna go to the Singles' Mingle so...

   J *is guiltily silent.*

ALEX. Oh my god. You're considering going, aren't you?

BIM. Don't be stupid –

J. A ticket's only a tenner, so I was thinking maybe...

BIM. Oh my god.

J. It's not... I just... it might get her off my case, y'know.

ALEX. Ah, I can't listen to this any more. This is bullshit.

J. Thanks for the support.

ALEX. I'm sorry, J, but it's true. What kind of friend would I be if I didn't tell you the truth?

J. The kind that listens.

ALEX. I have. And I'd be with you if you wanted to give up sex for you. But it's not what you want is it? You clearly want to sleep with that guy.

J. Who said that?

ALEX. It's written all over your face, babe.

BIM. It's true. Your nipples get erect just talking about him.

J. Well, maybe I do, and so? We can't always do what we want.

ALEX. But you can.

 J *doesn't respond.*

 ALEX *starts singing* (*badly*) *'Remember You' by The Weeknd and Wiz Khalifa.*

BIM. Did you actually just quote The Weeknd?

ALEX. What? There's some deep philosophy in those lyrics.

BIM. She actually has a point, J.

J. It's easy for you guys to say though. You can do whatever you want. (*To* ALEX.) You're already settled with Stephen. (*To* BIM.) And you haven't got your mum asking when are you going to bring a nice man home. And you've seen the WhatsApps my Aunt Mavis bombards me with. And that's only half of it. Whenever she gets invited to a wedding she uses it as an opportunity to ask when it'll be my turn. She thinks she's subtle. Now she's stopped saying anything and just sends me a picture of the bride and groom. It's just… (*Sighs.*) You know, the time I was in *Elle* she called me to say congratulations. And then said she was praying for me not to end up like Oprah. A billion-dollar empire but single.

BIM. But Oprah's not –

J. She's not married. To my family, it's the same thing.

ALEX. Aim for Oprah, b. Then you can pay for my kids' school fees.

J. You don't get it. The business, the flat, everything I'm proud of, it all means nothing, I mean nothing until I'm married.

BIM. So, this is about you finding someone?

J. Yes… no… no… not right now. Right now, I couldn't care less. But I'll want to settle down one day and I want to be able to prove them wrong. Show that I could do it all. I can make the salons a success and when I'm ready I can get the guy. I can have the lawyer or doctor that she desperately wants me to. And I can have everything I've ever wanted and I'll be enough. And I can. Just maybe not as I am. As I was. Because as my mum loves to remind me, nobody buys the cow if you can have the milk for free.

ALEX. Stephen did.

BIM. See, there's an exception to every rule.

J *is silent*.

J?

J *doesn't respond*.

J?

J *doesn't respond*.

ALEX. Babe, talk to us.

J. Why? You don't listen when I do.

ALEX. What are you talking about, we've just been listening to you.

J. No, you've just been hearing me speak. You never actually listen.

ALEX. Is there a difference?

J. Just forget it.

ALEX. Look, J, if this is who you really want to be, fine. Bim and I will accept it and we'll stop all the jokes and we'll support you in staying celibate. Bim will even join you for a month.

BIM *looks horrified*.

But if all this is because of your mum and Aunt Mavis – and I say this respectfully because I do love your mum and Aunt Mavis – tell them to go jump. It's your fucking life, J. Own it. Where's all your fire gone? J, you're the girl who told Samantha White that if she ever put a pen in your hair again, you'd leave her swinging from a tree.

J. She deserved it though.

ALEX. See, that's the J we know.

J. I'm still that girl.

ALEX. Then why doesn't it feel like it?

J. What are you trying to say?

ALEX. It's like you've lost your spark.

J. Are you saying I've got boring?

ALEX. That's not what I said.

J. But is it what you meant?

BIM. No, of course she didn't. She just meant that you're not as –

J. So you agree with her?

BIM *doesn't respond.*

Well, you're wrong. Okay, I'm not as carefree as you two and maybe my aunt is the reason I'm not having sex right now and maybe I should stand up to her but I haven't and maybe I will go the Singles' Mingle but none of that makes me boring. //

ALEX. Nobody said you were…

J. // Because if I was so boring would I have got my clit pierced?

ALEX *and* BIM *are in shock.*

ALEX. You did what?

BIM. Your mum is gonna kill you!

J. She's never gonna see it though.

BIM. Fucking hell. Did it hurt?

J. A little bit.

ALEX. When was this?

J. Last month.

BIM. What made you…

J. I was fed up of looking at Excel spreadsheets.

ALEX. And so you pierced your clit?

J. Something different.

ALEX. You've got some balls.

J. I told you I was still that girl.

BIM. I need to see it.

J. Okay.

J prepares to show the girls. BIM and ALEX gather round her and they continue talking as J gets ready.

BIM. I've heard that if it goes wrong you lose all feeling down there.

J. But when it goes right, everything is heightened.

BIM. Okay, missy!

She shows them the piercing and they react with squeals and screams. They inspect it for a while.

ALEX. So maybe I was wrong. Your spark is still there, it's just sitting firmly on your clit.

Scene Six

*Day eight. It's during the day and the girls are chilling in their
day outfits – think bikinis and kaftans.* ALEX *is in the toilet.* J *is
finishing plucking* BIM*'s chin hairs. Music is playing in the
background.*

J. Have you tried meditating?

BIM. I masturbate.

J. They're not the same thing.

BIM. Solo activity, nothing else needed, period of concentration
free from distractions and a feeling of ahhhh and relief after.

J. Yeah, I don't think it counts, Bim.

BIM. Why not? I masturbate as religiously as a Buddhist monk
meditates.

J. I'll be honest sometimes you speak and I can't help but laugh
because you're an Oxford grad. Like, you are actually in that
one per cent. Do you know how many rejects must be mad
that you got in instead of them?

BIM. What can I say? I'm multifaceted.

J. Geek in the streets and a freak in the sheets.

BIM. Basically.

J. I do love you.

BIM. Ah, babes, I love me too.

J. Bim, that's not how –

J's got a message on her phone.

The woman is back.

BIM. Your Aunt Mavis?

J. Who else? I didn't hear from her yesterday so I thought
maybe she was taking a break but nope. Now I have two to
make up for it. (*Reading the message.*) Oh my god! She's set
me up on a date for when I'm back. Look at him!

BIM. He looks like his personality is as dry as his lips.

J *groans*.

But he is a doctor.

J (*reading out the message*). 'I know you've been struggling to find someone yourself so thought this might help. Love Aunt Mavis. Kiss.'

BIM. You've got to give her credit for her persistence. She should consider starting a dating –

ALEX*'s phone starts ringing.* BIM *goes to get it whilst shouting for* ALEX.

(*Shouting to bathroom.*) Alex, your phone is ringing. It's Stephen. //

ALEX (*coming back into the room*). Don't pick up.

BIM (*picking up the call*). // I'll… Hey Stephen… no, it's Bim. Yeah, she's here. //

ALEX *starts shaking her head and signals for* BIM *to make out as if she's not around.*

// But she can't speak. She's… she's kinda busy right now… Yup, you know what she's like. She's been in the toilet for ages. Good luck when you guys move in together… Oh right okay… Yeah, I'll get Alex to message you… Alright, bye.

BIM *hangs up the call.*

What was that?

ALEX. What?

BIM. Making me lie to Stephen.

ALEX. I told you not to answer it. Dunno why you did.

BIM. Because he's your boyfriend and I thought you'd want to…

ALEX. Exactly. My boyfriend. So, if I told you to leave it, you should have left it. Dunno why you're obsessed with micromanaging everything.

BIM. I'm not.

J. You kinda are.

BIM. Shut up, J.

ALEX. What did he say anyway?

BIM. Wants to know what time we'll want picking up from the airport.

ALEX. Right.

BIM. Our flight lands at eight so you should probably tell him –

ALEX. It's fine, we'll get an Uber. I'll message him later.

BIM. Why would we do that?

ALEX. Because I wanna Uber back.

J. Is that the only reason?

ALEX. Yeah.

J. Nothing to do with wherever you went last night?

ALEX. When?

J. When you went missing for an hour.

BIM (*to* J). I thought we were gonna wait until lunch.

J. Well, we're talking about it now. Alex?

ALEX. What happens in Ibiza stays in Ibiza.

J. And we're still in Ibiza so you can tell us what happened.

ALEX *doesn't respond.*

BIM. Look, we all know you were with that barman.

ALEX. How?

BIM. You were doing your hungry eyes every time you looked at him and then you were gone for an hour.

ALEX. It wasn't an hour.

BIM. So you admit you were with him.

ALEX *is silent.*

J. Look, we already know you kissed him. We just wanna know exactly what happened.

ALEX. I didn't –

J. Alex, you're not fooling anyone. You definitely kissed him.

BIM. Babe, you were gone for so long you could have…

ALEX *looks guilty.* J *and* BIM *realise what* ALEX *is hiding.*

ALEX. That's what I was trying to say. I didn't just kiss him. We kinda…

J. Are you sure?

ALEX. Yeah, I'm pretty sure, J.

J. But I thought you were on your period.

ALEX. And?

J. Oh, wow.

BIM. So did it look like a crime scene after?

ALEX. Don't I feel shit enough as it is. I don't even know why… y'know, I knew it was wrong. As soon as we kissed I said 'Alex, stop.' When he put his fingers inside I said, 'Alex, stop.' And then he was there with his head between my thighs and I knew I should tell him to stop… but I held his head tighter instead. And it felt so good. His tongue… my clit… all the months of craving just started to fade away. And then he was inside me and I came and reality came shitting on my parade. And he's there looking at me asking me how it was and all I could think about was Stephen. And okay so, I'm not in love with him. But I do love him. And maybe one day I would have got there. But I fucked up.

BIM. Where did this even –

J *hits* BIM *to get her to shut up.*

J. Okay, this isn't great but couples have got through worse and Stephen loves you.

ALEX. I'm not telling him!

BIM. Alex, you can't lie to him.

ALEX. It's not a lie, just an omission.

J. A drunken kiss you can omit but this…

ALEX. Was just drunken sex.

J. Just?

BIM. Alex, he has a right to know.

ALEX. I can't.

BIM. So you're just going to bury your head in the sand?

ALEX. Look, I don't wanna–

J. It can't always be about what you want.

ALEX. Isn't it my life?

BIM. But there are other people in it. You forget that.

J. You forgot that.

ALEX. I didn't forget. I just…

BIM. Honesty is the best policy. It won't necessarily be an easy conversation –

ALEX. Yeah. And sometimes you're not ready to have those difficult conversations. (*To* BIM.) You of all people know what that's like.

BIM. Why are you bringing it up again?

J. Something tells me we're no longer taking about last night.

Silence.

What's going on?

BIM. Nothing.

J asks again with her face.

It's nothing.

ALEX. Stop being so dismissive about this. It's not nothing.

BIM. That's a bit rich coming from you.

ALEX. Okay, I take that. But it's not nothing, Bim. You…

J. Okay, can somebody please tell me what you two are talking about?

Silence.

Alex?

ALEX. It's not for me to say.

J. Bim?

ALEX. Tell her.

J. Tell me what?

ALEX. Honesty is the best policy.

BIM. I'm going toilet.

J *blocks her path.*

J. No, you're going to tell me what's going on.

BIM. I told Alex something and she's just a bit sensitive about it.

J. Okay, told her something about what?

BIM. The night I went to hospital.

J. When you got your stomach pumped?

BIM. Yeah. /

ALEX. She made that up. It never happened.

BIM *shoots* ALEX *a look.*

J. You didn't go to the hospital or you didn't get your stomach pumped?

BIM. I went to the hospital, I just didn't…

J. So why where you there, Bim?

BIM. Why am I being interrogated when I wasn't the one who cheated last night?

J. Why were you there, Bim?

BIM. I said, it's nothing.

J. Well, it's clearly not nothing because Alex is still upset about it.

BIM. Yeah, well she's being dramatic.

ALEX. I'm not being –

J. If it's nothing, then why can't you just say? And if it's something then… you're making me nervous. Please, Bim, just tell me what's going on.

BIM *realises she's going to have to tell the truth and gathers herself to do so.*

BIM. I took an overdose, now can we move on?

J. You…

BIM. Would you rather eat chocolate that tastes like poo or poo that tastes like chocolate?

J. What?

BIM. I heard one of the guys ask it last night. It's quite the conundrum, isn't it? //

J. Bim, you can't just change topic like that.

BIM. // I mean it begs all sorts of questions really. Because if the poo tastes like chocolate is it really poo? //

J. Bim, can you stop ignoring me?

BIM. // Is it not just chocolate produced in a –

J. Bim, I'm not going to go away.

BIM *accepts her tactic isn't working.*

Why didn't you say?

BIM. I did. I told Alex.

ALEX. Bim, c'mon. This happened three months ago and you only told me a few days before we flew out and only because your mum made you. You had no intention of saying anything otherwise.

BIM. Well, can you blame me? It's not exactly the sort of thing you want to just call someone up and say. 'Hiya, how's things? Yeah I'm okay. Just been working, spending some time with the family and oh yeah, I tried to take my life yesterday.' Bit of a moodkiller really. Plus, I knew if I said, you wouldn't have agreed to Ibiza.

J. That's not –

BIM *looks at* J. *They both know* BIM *is right.* J *concedes defeat.*

BIM. Exactly, and I needed this trip.

ALEX. Well, if it was a holiday you wanted we could have just gone somewhere calm like – (*Pronouncing 'Nice' like 'nice', the word meaning 'pleasant'.*) Nice.

J (*pronouncing 'Nice' like the French city*). Nice.

BIM. Nice would have been too easy. Ibiza's… Ibiza. And I wanted to prove to myself I could handle being here, without any help from anyone or anything.

J. Bim, I'm –

BIM. You never answered the question, J. Chocolate poo or poo-flavoured chocolate?

J. Chocolate… I… I dunno. Sorry, I'm still –

BIM. See. Moodkiller.

J. No, it's just… it's… what happened, Bim?

BIM. I dunno. It just… It was just dark. But I wasn't trying to… I just needed the pain to stop.

J. Why didn't you tell us any of this?

BIM. What could you have said?

ALEX. We love you, maybe.

BIM. Sometimes love isn't enough.

J. What about now?

BIM. What do you mean?

J. Well, you seem fine. But before you seemed… y'know, you were always laughing.

BIM. I'm okay. That night… I guess it kind of gave me hope. There was this nurse. (*Tracing the imaginary scars on her arm*.) And she had these scars… said she'd been to the dark places too. And she was the first person I'd met who really understood. But she was fine now. She had a baby daughter and her scars, they were… they were just that – healed wounds, relics from the past. And she told me I didn't need to die to be reborn. She made me believe it was possible. So I decided I wasn't going to give up.

J. Were you scared…

BIM. Not like now. Deciding to live but not knowing how. But I'm trying. We're in Ibiza, after all.

J. I'm just glad…

J *hugs* BIM *and* ALEX *joins in.*

ALEX. You know we love you, right?

J. So much.

BIM. Does that mean now's a good time to tell you I hate that dress you wanna wear tonight?

ALEX. What?

BIM. Alex, it's ugly, man. The shoes too.

ALEX. There's nothing wrong –

BIM. At least we won't have to worry about you running off with any more men. Nobody will go near you in that.

ALEX. Bim!

BIM. You love me, remember. Love. Love. Love.

Scene Seven

Day nine. 6 p.m. The girls are almost ready to go out. BIM *is in the bathroom.* ALEX *is finishing* J's *make-up. They are going to The Zoo Project and are wearing animal print.*

ALEX. Done.

J (*looking in a mirror*). I didn't think it was possible but I think I've got better looking since we've been out here.

ALEX. It's the sun.

J is taking selfies and admiring each one.

J. To be this fit, smart and successful should be a crime. I don't know why my Aunt Mavis is worried. Any man would be lucky to have me.

ALEX. That's what we've been trying to tell you all holiday!

J. It's a shame we've only got two more nights left. Feels like Ibiza hasn't really seen me.

ALEX. Trust me, we can make up for it in two nights. Why don't we go to Ibiza Rocks first for drinks and then –

J. We were there last night.

ALEX. Yeah, I know. But it's quite nice in there so I thought –

J. You wanna see that barman again, don't you?

ALEX. No... I just... I mean he said, if we came back he could do us all drinks on the house.

J. Oh, well that makes it alright then.

ALEX. Oh c'mon, J. Just one drink.

J. And another fumble?

ALEX. J!

J. Your guilty conscience evaporated very quickly.

ALEX. That's not true. I do feel bad but I also feel really alive and I haven't felt that in ages. I just wanna hold on to that for a little bit longer.

J. We're not going, Alex. You're still with Stephen, I'm not gonna be an –

ALEX. So, I'll break up with him.

J. What?

ALEX. Well, you won't let us go to Ibiza Rocks otherwise, so I'll end it now.

J. Now? Alex, you're being stupid, this is –

ALEX. I've made up my mind.

ALEX *gets her phone.*

J. If you want to break up with him, fine, but don't do it like this.

ALEX (*practising what she's going to say*). 'Hiya!' No. Too cheery.

J. Just think about him for a second.

ALEX. 'Hey, hun, have you got a moment?' That's not it.

J. This is Stephen. He deserves better than this.

ALEX. Mmm... 'Can we talk?' Fuck it! I'm just gonna freestyle.

ALEX *goes to call Stephen. She's about to press the call button. She freezes. She can't do it. J goes to take the phone from her.* ALEX *doesn't resist.*

I'm gonna have to talk to him when I get back, aren't I?

J *nods.*

What will I even say? Fuck's sake, Alex. Why did you have to be so stupid?

J. Babe, it's done now. You're doing the right thing by telling him but –

ALEX. It's gonna break his heart.

J. Maybe. But you didn't mean to hurt him. You were just... Look, I'll help you work out how to tell Stephen when we're back. But right now, we're in Ibiza. You can't do anything about it. So let's make the most of our last couple of nights like you said. I mean, babe, Zoo Project!

ALEX. You're right. You know I began planning my outfit for tonight as soon as we booked our –

BIM *enters from the bathroom. She isn't dressed.*

J. Babe, you're not dressed.

BIM. Yeah, I'm not coming out. I don't feel up to it.

J. So, we'll stay in.

BIM. No. It's fine.

ALEX. Bim, we're not leaving you.

BIM. I'm asking you to. Look I'm fine. It's just…

J. Exactly, more reason why we should –

BIM. I don't need babysitting! It'll pass, I just need to take it easy, get some sleep and not drink.

J looks unsure.

J, I'm not gonna top myself. Been there done that, got the T-shirt. Plus, can you imagine the headlines. Essex girl found dead in Ibiza. Tragic.

ALEX. They wouldn't put you in the papers though. They don't put us in the news unless we've been stabbed or you're Beyoncé.

BIM. Even more reason not to do it then. I wouldn't even get my fifteen minutes of fame.

J. How can you just joke about it?

BIM. Because it's my life, J. What should I do? Cry?

BIM *starts flicking through a magazine.* J *and* ALEX *don't move.*

Look, go out. I'll be fine.

ALEX. I'm just worried in case… I mean what if someone –

BIM. I'm in the hotel room. I'm safer here than when I'm out there running off with every Tom, Dick and Harry, and you don't worry about me then.

ALEX. I do. Gonorrhoea is up one hundred and twenty-three per cent.

BIM. Condoms, Alex. Look, I promise I'll call you both if it gets really bad. But right now, I'm ordering you to go.

Silence.

Guys, please. Do you know how bad I'd feel if you missed out on The Zoo Project because of me?

J. You promise you'll call us?

BIM. I promise.

J. We'll text you as well, and you can keep us updated on how you're feeling.

BIM. J, that's a bit... Fine.

ALEX. And let us know when you go to sleep so we don't worry.

BIM. Yes, Mum.

J. Okay, we'll go.

BIM. Good. Because there is alcohol to be drank and men to be danced on.

J. Don't think Alex needs any encouragement in that department.

BIM. Yeah, the men are for J, Alex, not you.

J. We'll do you proud.

BIM. I look forward to hearing the stories.

BIM *hypes* J *and* ALEX *up as they say goodbye and leave.* BIM *waits for a moment to make sure they're not coming back. As she goes to sit down her physical bravado falls and it's clear from the way she holds her body that she is feeling worse than she indicated. She is agitated once again. Her fight with her hands is even more aggressive. She is losing control quickly. She breathes in deeply and starts talking to herself again.*

No, no, no, no, no. This isn't how it's supposed to be. No. No. I'm fine. I've got this. I'm fine. I'm...

BIM *cries out in frustration and starts hitting her head with her fists. It goes on for longer this time. As she's lashing out, her phone rings twice but she ignores it or doesn't notice. After a while she comes to and realises what she's been doing and regular* BIM *returns. She is silent for a short period afterwards and silently stares into space. She goes to get her tablets. She considers taking all of them. Her phone rings again. She sighs. It's apparent the person isn't going away. She picks up.*

Hey, Chris… Yeah sorry, about that I was in the shower. What's up… Oh, you spoke to Alex… Nah, you're alright… I'm just run down, I'm fine… Okay fine, you can come hang for a bit but you have to promise me you'll still go out after. I don't want to ruin anyone's night… Okay. See you in a bit. Just call me when you're here.

BIM *hangs up the call.*

(*Psyching herself up to be in company.*) You've got this. You've got this.

Scene Eight

Day ten. The three girls are discussing the events of last night. BIM *is holding Dress B to give it to* J, *who snatches it gleefully from her hands.*

ALEX. So, you mean you just let me sleep on Chris cum?

BIM. You're assuming we didn't use a condom.

J. There's also pre-cum.

BIM. Shut up, J.

ALEX. Condom or no condom, that's gross, Bim.

BIM. Alex, I'm sorry. Look, I promise if you get pregnant by Chris's pre-cum I'll help you take care of the baby.

J *and* BIM *laugh.*

ALEX. You're not funny.

BIM. I know, I'm hilarious.

ALEX. No. You're annoying. But I am glad to see you're in a better mood than last night.

J. Guess we've got Chris to thank for that.

ALEX. So much for a quiet night in.

BIM. That is what I had planned. This just kinda happened.

ALEX. Sex doesn't just happen, Bim. Especially not with you. And you're always going on about how tight you are, so I doubt he just fell into your vagina.

BIM. I dunno, Alex, it just –

J. Where there's a will-y, there's a way.

BIM. Shut up, J!

J starts dancing round BIM, *waving the dress about.*

J. Don't get mad at me because you lost the bet. Have a word with your – (*Points at her vagina.*) about that. She's your Judas.

BIM. You're so annoyingly happy right now.

J. Sore loser, are we?

BIM *ignores* J.

I'm gonna wear this dress tonight so every time you look at me you remember I won.

BIM. You know sometimes, J, I really hate you.

J. Don't worry this glee isn't reserved for you only. I decided to end my sex sabbatical last night.

BIM. Did you sleep with the guy?

J. Which guy?

BIM. Y'know.

ALEX. She means the one that makes your nipples stand to attention.

J. Turns out he doesn't believe in sex before marriage. What a joke! One should always try before they buy.

BIM. What would your Aunt Mavis say?

J. Fuck Aunt Mavis!

ALEX *and* BIM *are stunned.*

ALEX. What?

J. You heard me. I am done with that woman's nonsense.

J *picks up her phone.*

I'm gonna block her.

BIM. You're not!

J. Watch me.

BIM *and* ALEX *gather round* J *excitedly. They scream with excitement as she blocks her.*

And I'm going to tell her that if she wants to be a part of my life then she just has to back off.

ALEX. Well…

BIM. More of this J, please. Where has she been all holiday?

J. I know. (*Looking at* ALEX.) But sometimes you just need reminding who you are. And despite what my mum or my Aunt Mavis say, I'm fucking awesome and no amount of sex can take that away from me.

ALEX *and* BIM *respond with more cheers of encouragement.*

And so I've scheduled two dick appointments for when we get back.

BIM. Already?

J. Well, I've got a lot of catching up to do. Even thought to send them both a little teaser.

ALEX. J!

BIM. I thought your nudes were for you.

J. It'd be selfish of me not to share, wouldn't it. (*Looking at the photos*.) Which one do you think?

BIM. That one. It'd make me wanna sleep with you.

J (*sending the photo*). Done.

ALEX. Yes, girl.

BIM. I feel like we should be having a toast.

J (*grabbing her stuff for the shower and heading towards the bath*). Trust me, as soon as I've showered, we will be celebrating my return to hoe-dom.

ALEX. J, where are you going? You know I said I was going in –

J *exits for the shower.*

(*So J can hear in the bathroom.*) Bitch!

BIM *is lost in her thoughts.* ALEX *is deciding what to wear. She catches sight of* BIM *a couple of times as she does so, and begins to suspect something's not right.*

You okay?

BIM. Huh?

ALEX. Are you okay?

BIM. Yeah, yeah, I'm fine. Just tired.

ALEX. Because you spent last night doing bedroom gymnastics instead of resting like you were supposed to.

BIM. Alright, Alex.

ALEX. I was joking, Bim.

Silence.

BIM. We didn't use a condom.

ALEX *goes to respond.*

Don't.

ALEX. Do you want me to find out where we can get the morning-after pill out here?

BIM *is silent.*

Bim?

BIM. I'm just annoyed with myself because I know better than that.

ALEX. Don't beat yourself up about it. We've all done it once.

BIM *doesn't respond.*

And at least it was with Chris – he's a good guy, he's unlikely to have anything. But I'll go with you to get tested when we're back. Ooh, we can go to the one in Central. I've forgotten the name but it's nice there. You get free tea and coffee and everything. It's like The Savoy of sex clinics. Bim?

As BIM speaks, ALEX realises what happened last night, though BIM shows no sign of thinking anything was wrong.

BIM. It just… it all just happened so quickly. One minute I'm convincing you guys to go out, the next Chris is about to go in. But we were never supposed… just cuddling escalated very quickly. And I'd said 'wait' but you know what he's like. Took it personally. Went on all affronted till I told him it wasn't about him. And then he kissed me, and we're kissing and then… well, then he was inside. And I… I didn't stop him.

ALEX. But, Bim, you didn't say yes.

Scene Nine

A couple of hours later. BIM *is in the shower.* ALEX *and* J *are mindful as they speak that she doesn't overhear them. Dress B is on* J*'s side.*

J. Look, maybe there's nothing to say. I mean this is Chris we're talking about. He's hardly a… And Bim's, well, Bim. No one can get her to do anything she doesn't want to do – ever. She's basically a dominatrix, just with less leather. If they had sex then –

ALEX. J, she didn't say yes.

J. But she never actually said no.

ALEX. She said wait.

J. Does that mean no?

ALEX. Does it sound like it meant yes?

Silence.

I know Bim, J. She didn't want it.

J. And you think Chris knew that too?

ALEX. He's an intelligent boy with functioning ears and he never heard her say yes. If he can get a first from Oxford, he can deduce what that meant.

J. But how many times do you actively say yes to sex, Alex? This whole 'wait for yes for consent' thing only works in textbooks. It's not made for real life. I mean when you first slept with Stephen did he really stop to ask you if you definitely wanted to do it?

Silence.

And before he went in did you ever actually say, 'yes, I want this'?

Silence.

Exactly. It's more complicated than a simple yes and no, Alex.

ALEX. But just think about what you said just now. Bim is basically a dominatrix; she lives for power. She makes mini-plans of actions for even her one-night stands. So how comes this 'just happened'?

J. Okay maybe she didn't plan it but stuff like this happens to us all the time. It doesn't make it, y'know. Like when you're not a hundred per cent in the mood with a guy, and he convinces you to just let him put the tip in. But it's never just the tip, ever, and before you know it he's all up in your insides and you're having sex. You didn't necessarily want it but now he's there you just go with it, you let it happen. And y'know we always end up laughing about it the next time we catch up.

ALEX. J, what part of that sounds right to you? It's not okay, let's be honest. We make jokes so we don't have to face the facts. We weren't in control. And so maybe it wasn't violent and it was shrouded with caresses and compliments and maybe we didn't say no, maybe we said 'I'm not sure', 'wait' or maybe we said nothing and our bodies tensed up but we didn't want it. When he goes in with 'just the tip', you don't want it. And Bim didn't want it.

J. I can't, Alex, I can't believe that Chris –

ALEX. They didn't use a condom, J! Does that really sound like Bim to you?

J. They…

ALEX *shakes her head. It sinks in for* J.

Oh, Bim.

ALEX. I know.

J. I really, really didn't want to believe you were right…

Silence.

What do we do?

ALEX. I dunno. Guess it's up to her.

J. Does she…

ALEX. I think a part of her knows. I've never heard her speak about sex with regret before but earlier… There was just something about the way she spoke. I don't think she's okay with what happened.

BIM *enters from the shower.* ALEX *and* J *look at each other.* BIM *picks up on the tension.*

BIM. What's going on?

ALEX. Nothing.

BIM. Well, can you both stop looking so miserable then. It's killing my vibe.

ALEX. Sorry.

J. Can we talk?

BIM. That is what I've been doing.

J. Yeah… I guess… I just…

BIM. What have you done, J? Did you lose my lipstick? I knew I shouldn't have lent it to –

J. No. It's… just about last night…

J *can't find the words so awkwardly tries to hand Dress B back to* BIM.

Chris went in without a condom?

BIM *shoots a look at* ALEX.

Look, I'm not judging you. We all know I've had my fair share of unprotected sex. But you're so anal about them It just –

BIM. Sometimes the hoe just takes over.

J. Right.

Silence.

ALEX. You know you can talk to us.

BIM. Thanks for the offer but don't think I can afford another therapist.

ALEX. I'm being serious.

BIM. So was I.

ALEX *considers leaving the conversation but changes her mind. She tries to find the right words.*

ALEX. What happened last night… that… that wasn't right. You didn't want to have sex.

BIM. Well, it wasn't exactly how I planned my evening but –

ALEX. Chris, shouldn't have –

BIM. Stop.

ALEX. You said wait and he still went in.

BIM *is silent.*

Bim, you said wait.

As BIM *talks she slowly faces up to what happened. Hurt and confusion can be detected but she doesn't become tearful nor does she ever breakdown completely in distress. If anything, she is numb, speaking matter-of-factly as if she's discussing something more routine. When she starts to feel overwhelmed by the severity of the discussion she tries to inject some humour.*

BIM. Exactly. I only said wait. That could have meant anything. Y'know, it can mean 'oh wait, get a condom'. Or 'wait, go over there'. Or 'wait… wait… please wait. I don't want this to happen'. And I… I didn't want it to happen. But it did. And he didn't even use a condom and I… well I… I still don't know how that happened. To me. With my friend. I did think about saying no. I thought about saying 'stop, get out' – (*Trying to be light-hearted.*) 'I didn't actually say you could go in there' but I mean once it starts you can't exactly stop it, can you? It's a bit of a faux pas, y'know. You just have to… you just go with it, don't you? I mean you would have too, right? But I'm sure if I'd… I'm sure if I'd said 'Stop,' I'm sure if I'd said 'No, no, don't, I don't want it.' I'm sure if I said that, he would have stopped. But I didn't. Because I'm not one hundred per cent sure that he would have. And if he didn't then I would have had to accept that I was powerless. And that… No. So, I just let it happen.

Because that way, at least in my head, I was still in control, y'know.

The girls go to comfort BIM. *She resists. Silence as they all reflect on what has happened.*

J. What do you wanna do?

BIM. I just want to get drunk and enjoy my last night.

BIM *puts some music on. She gathers the shot glasses and tequila rosé and starts pouring shots.*

ALEX. Bim, I don't think that's a good id–

BIM. Maybe it's not but it's what I want.

BIM *tries to hand the girls a shot glass each but they don't take it.*

J. So we're just supposed to forget –

BIM. Yes. Look I don't know… but for now, I just want us to forget about it. Okay?

BIM *urges them again to take a shot glass.* ALEX *and* J *don't take it.*

Guys, please! Let me forget about it. Please. For me.

ALEX *and* J *each take a glass from* BIM *but they don't go to drink it. The three stand there looking at each other.* J *and* ALEX *are clearly uncomfortable with what's going on.*

ALEX. Bim…

BIM. I'm good.

A moment. It's clear to the girls she's not. But it's also clear to them that this is the only way she's prepared to move forward.

ALEX. Okay. We'll do this, we'll do tonight, however you want. But you've got to promise us, and I mean promise us, that we're gonna deal with this when we get home. I don't know how but… when we're back, we've got to talk about this. Okay?

BIM. Okay, I promise. (*Raising her shot glass*.) Now, to us. The three hoes of Essex.

ALEX and J *lack* BIM*'s enthusiasm in saying the next line.*

ALL. The three hoes of Essex!

They all down the shot and slam it down. BIM *picks up Dress B from where* J *left it. She holds it, clearly unsettled.*

Scene Ten

That night. BIM *is in the hotel room alone. She left the club early without* J *and* ALEX. *Dress B is back on* BIM*'s side. She is in the middle of one of her violent outbursts and is hitting herself.* J *and* ALEX *enter as the scene begins but* BIM *doesn't notice. It's the first time they've seen her like this. They are hesitant. Scared to approach.*

ALEX. Bim?

BIM *keeps hitting herself, in her trance. Unaware.*

Bim! Please, stop.

BIM *stops. Not as a reaction to* ALEX*'s plea but because the feeling has passed. The spell is broken and she slowly comes to her senses, staring into space. She is still unresponsive to* ALEX *and* J.

J. Bim, it's us. We're here.

BIM *acknowledges the girls.*

ALEX. What was that, Bim?

BIM *shrugs. She can't explain it. The girls don't push it. They move on.*

J. Are you alright?

BIM *nods but is clearly not okay.*

ALEX. Do you wanna talk about it?

BIM *shakes her head, but without further prompting starts speaking anyway.*

BIM. It's just I've been trying so hard, y'know to be… and this was the one thing it felt like I had any control over and he… And seeing him tonight just…

J. You saw him?

ALEX. I knew we shouldn't have gone out.

BIM. No, it's fine. I wanted to.

J. Did he say anything to you about…

BIM *shakes her head.*

BIM. He just spoke like nothing had happened. But he sensed I was being funny with him and wanted to know why.

J. What did you say?

BIM. Nothing. I tried… but the words… I couldn't. I couldn't even look at him. But I wanted to and I was really hoping I could. Because we're all going to Oxford in a couple of weeks and I'll have to look at him then and this… this will have to be normal. But when he was there, in front of me, it was just… I dunno… And I can see him looking at me getting frustrated and I'm frustrated because I can't tell him… I can't tell him that he hurt me. And I felt my eyes starting to sting and I was not about to be that girl, so I left.

J. Bim…

BIM *senses the girls are worried about her.*

BIM. I'm fine. Trust me. Think I might join you vibrator shopping though. I reckon it'll be a while until y'know I'm up to rolling around with men again. But I still have needs. And when you've got an A-class vagina like mine it needs tending to and looking after.

J (*laughing*). Bim…

ALEX. You're such an idiot.

BIM. Your favourite idiot.

J. I'll come with you but I won't be getting one for myself. Now I'm over this sex ban I can have the real thing. And I can't wait!

ALEX. Who said you can't do both? I have three vibrators and a boyfriend. Had a boyfriend. I'll probably need a fourth to replace Stephen so I'll come too.

BIM. Oh, babes.

J. You might still be able to work things out.

ALEX. I don't want us to. I'll miss him but if I'm honest with myself, he's not right for me. And I've known that for a while. I just liked the convenience of it all.

A sad silence falls upon them. After some time, J *gets up decisively.*

J. Nope. This is not how we're spending our last night.

J *runs to put a song on with excitement. Crazy Cousins featuring Mc Versatile 'The Funky Anthem' begins. The mood lifts instantly and the girls get up energised by the song. They start dancing, their moves building with the music.*

BIM. Yes, J!

ALEX. This song gives me all of the Napa feels.

BIM. It's like being eighteen again.

The girls continue dancing, and start singing along.

J. It's the funky anthem.

ALEX. Crazy Cousinz.

BIM. Mc Versatile.

ALL. North, east, south, west.

J. London.

BIM. Manchester, Birmingham, Coventry.

ALEX. UK.

ALL. The world.

As the beat drops the girls start skanking fully, taking themselves back to Napa, back to being eighteen, back to being carefree. They sing along as they dance and the joy is palpable. After some time, BIM *slowly withdraws from the singing and dancing as she comes back to reality, and she simply watches* ALEX *and* J, *who don't notice at first. As they continue she starts to become overwhelmed with emotion. After a while,* ALEX *and* J *each notice* BIM'*s absence and their singing breaks off as does their dancing.*

J. Bim?

BIM (*visibly upset*). No, it's alright. I'm fine. I'm just… I'm not fine.

The girls go to comfort BIM.

ALEX. Oh, Bim.

BIM. It's okay.

J. It's not though, is it?

BIM. No it's not… not right now. But I can survive this, right? All of it. Got that Nigerian resilience, haven't I? So whatever it takes… I'm gonna get there.

J. Of course, you will.

ALEX. You've got us.

BIM. And soon I'll have my new vibrator.

ALEX *and* J *look at* BIM.

What? You guys can't do everything for me.

ALEX. We were having a sentimental moment.

BIM. My vagina doesn't know sentiments, guys.

J. You're actually such a hoe.

BIM. And proud of it.

End of play.